Sales

Sales Strategies

The Top 100 Best Ways To Increase Sales

By Ace McCloud
Copyright © 2015

Disclaimer

The information provided in this book is designed to provide helpful information on the subjects discussed. This book is not meant to be used, nor should it be used, to diagnose or treat any medical condition. For diagnosis or treatment of any medical problem, consult your own physician. The publisher and author are not responsible for any specific health or allergy needs that may require medical supervision and are not liable for any damages or negative consequences from any treatment, action, application or preparation, to any person reading or following the information in this book. Any references included are provided for informational purposes only. Readers should be aware that any websites or links listed in this book may change.

Table of Contents

DEDICATED TO THOSE WHO ARE PLAYING THE GAME OF LIFE TO

WIN

KEEP ON PUSHING AND NEVER GIVE UP!

Ace McCloud

Be sure to check out my website for all my Books and Audio books.

www.AcesEbooks.com

Introduction

I want to thank you and congratulate you for buying the book, "Sales: The Top 100 Best Ways to Increase Sales."

A career in sales and selling can often be tricky. In the past, selling was relatively easy thanks to television/radio and big-name corporations establishing the roots for some of the most popular products and services that many households still rely on today. However, marketing strategies have changed over time and the world has gotten increasingly smarter. While it was fairly easy to sell things in the past with fewer regulations, limited information and less competition, today consumers are smarter, more skeptical and much more willing to do research and search around for the best deals. Technology has also had a huge impact on sales and selling—for example, companies can no longer trick consumers into buying shoddy products because most unhappy consumers will complain on social media, leave bad reviews and spread the word about how unhappy they are with a product, thus killing sales for that particular company. This is why it is so important to utilize all the information you will learn in this book so that you can excel were others will fall flat on their face.

Over the years, the term "Sales Person" has taken on a negative connotation for many people due to the few who have really done their customers a disservice in a variety of ways. You might even share this same viewpoint due to some bad experiences you may have had in the past. What do you think of when you hear the word "Salesman"? An image of a pushy car salesman who is only looking out for himself comes to mind for most people. While this stereotype does no justice for the hardworking men and women who have careers in sales today, it still tends to have a negative effect on the attitude that consumers have toward this profession. That attitude is what often makes working in sales challenging.

If you're working in sales, that attitude leaves you with two options: You can either give up or you can do what is right and truly help consumers to get the product that they need while making a nice income for yourself. Sales are what make the world go round and it can be an extremely exciting and satisfying profession in which you can make a lot of money.

Your mission as a salesperson is to help challenge the stereotype of salespeople that consumers have as a way to maximize customer trust and increase your sales and income. By doing this, you can make your job less stressful, make some new friends and grow your bank account while providing the client with remarkable service that will have them coming back to you time and time again with maybe even some nice referrals as well. Many people are turned off from careers in sales because they think that it's just way too hard, but that is hardly the case—as long as you have a strategy and a good attitude, a career in sales can be long, rewarding and after you have laid the foundation, even "easy."

This book contains proven steps and strategies on how to increase your sales by focusing on the most important areas of selling, such as customer service and marketing, as well as areas of personal development for you as a salesperson. As you read through this book, you will discover how to get into the minds of your consumers so that you can provide them with what they want and leave them happy they purchased from you. A rule of thumb in sales and marketing is that you must provide clients with what they *want*, not necessarily what they *need*, because consumers will often buy the basic versions of what they need but they are often times willing to spend more money to get the things they *desire*.

I was in the sales profession for over twenty years before I became an author and I learned a lot over that time! I have been in the trenches with cell phones and fitness memberships to being with huge companies that spared no expense but demanded excellence. I have had Fortune 500 companies, such as Wells Fargo; spend thousands of dollars bringing me to the best training programs in the world. I have also studied diligently on this subject for many years and put the strategies that you are about to learn into practice very successfully. Most importantly, I have been a consistent top producer with countless #1 for the month trophies. By utilizing just a few of the techniques you will discover in this book you should be able to significantly increase your sales the right way so that you can build up your reputation and bank account as well!

Chapter 1: The Top 100 Best Ways to Increase Sales

Strategy

This chapter will list the top 100+ tips, tricks and strategies that you can utilize to increase *your* chances of closing more sales and making more money. As always, it all comes down to planning and strategy. Feel free to experiment with the ideas listed in this chapter to see which ones work best for you and your market of clients. I also encourage you to experiment with them to see which ones work best together for your particular field and personality. Sales is a broad career so there is no "one-size-fits-all" answer—what works best for you will depend on your market, your personal strengths and what you're selling. Get ready to discover some of the best secrets that you can use to help you close more deals!

Stay on Top of Trends

Trending topics are taking over the world! Trending topics are called "trending" because they go viral for a short period of time before people eventually stop the buzz. If you have a Facebook and/or Twitter account you can see what topics are trending by looking right at your homepages. You can also find out what topics are trending by reading the news or using Google Trends.

The good thing about trending topics is that you can strategically use them to market and gain sales. For example, one of the trending topics (according to Facebook) at the time of this writing is #KissAGingerDay, a topic revolving around giving affection to redheads. Let's pretend that you are a marketer who is in charge of stirring up commotion for your company's Valentine's Day products. Since #KissAGingerDay is related to love and affection, you could integrate it into your marketing strategy and increase the chances of people seeing your content, because that's what they're searching for—that's what the buzz is around right now.

Trends have made some companies turn rich overnight (not really, but almost). For example, think about the leaders in Internet connectivity (AOL, DSL, Cable, etc.) and the leaders in technology (from flip phones to iPhones and from VHS players to Blu-Ray players). The great thing about trending topics is that nearly everyone is interested at the time of the trend—however there is one factor that you must be very aware of when dealing with trends: **Eventually that trend will fall off.**

Remember when DVDs came out? Each disc cost about $25 and it caused companies to start selling VHS tapes at a fraction of the cost. These days, due to newer services like Netflix (a streaming movie rental website) and Hulu Plus (similar), you can walk into a store and usually see a big bin of DVDs marked down to as low as $1! The same goes for those mom-and-pop video rental stores—with newer services like Redbox (an automated $1/night DVD rental kiosk found in most grocery stores) and Movies On Demand with just the touch of the button on your TV remote control, the days of super profitable video rental stores are long gone.

The moral of the story is that you always have to be vigilant of rapidly changing trends if you're going to use them to generate sales. You can't get used to status quo when it comes to this. The CEO of Netflix may be doing well now but he or she had better plan on staying on top of trends if Netflix wants to have a chance in the future. If you get too comfortable with the sales you generate off a current trend, you're likely going to be in for a rude awakening when your competitor figures out what the "next big thing" is and hops on it before you do.

Challenge Everyone's Comfort Level

As a person who works in sales or whose job it is to generate sales, you already know how tricky it can be to accomplish your sales goals sometimes. Have you ever thought about just *why* sales can be so tricky? The answer is really simple—people become comfortable and happy with what they have already. Many of those working in sales believe the problem is that people are not willing to pay money for things that they don't need—but that couldn't be further from the truth! In fact, some people are willing to pay top dollar for the best of the best in terms of something that can help them get to where they want to be.

The real problem is one for you to solve. The best way to generate sales is to challenge the status quo of your clients. Your clients are happy with what they have, hence the reason they haven't come running to you. Your job is to challenge this mindset, get into your clients' heads and start piquing their interests. It sounds hard but it's actually real easy... all you have to do is put yourself in your client's shoes.

The first step is to find out what your client *wants*... not what he or she needs, but what he or she really *wants*. This is usually the #1 mistake that people in sales are taught. A client who needs something will go out and get it and it won't matter where it's from. You wake up and your teeth are feeling nasty—you *need* toothpaste—it won't matter if it's Crest, Aim or some generic brand. You haven't eaten all day and you're hungry—you need to eat—and you'll probably go for whatever you can get, it doesn't matter whether it's a home-cooked meal, McDonalds, or a frozen dinner if that is what is the closest and most convenient. Even when it comes down to love... people need to feel love and affection and sometimes they will look for it anywhere. You may be thinking, "If I were in these scenarios, I wouldn't go for the first thing that I could get to fulfill my needs, I would go for brand x or brand y." **That** is the key here—people have needs and they want to fulfil them with what they *prefer*. That's where the loophole exists. You need to brush your teeth but maybe there is a certain brand you prefer because of the ingredients or anti-cavity properties... you need to eat but maybe you prefer something healthy because it is aligned with your health beliefs, etc.

Now do you see why people are willing to pay good money for something they *want* versus something they just need? People who believe that organic/gluten-free is healthier have no problem paying extra for those products. Hardcore industry leaders have no problem paying top dollar for a coach to teach them the best ways to get ahead in new areas of technology. Huge corporations are willing to spend tens of thousands of dollars to train their people to be super human salespeople. This mentality ranges from young to old—kids who want to be "in" have no problem saving up their money for the most expensive pack of trading cards that everyone is playing with and some people have no problem buying the rarest and fanciest of cars that are worth more than most houses. You need to be sure to explain why your product/service is the "BEST" and how happy the customer would be having it.

Most of the time, nobody will express interest until you or someone challenges their comfort level. For example, let's pretend you're a business coach who is pretty well-off... you're well-known in the community, you have no problem getting referrals and recommendations, you've had a good education and you have more certifications than anyone you know, etc. Let's Say that you were doing fine until you saw a business coach advertising for a social media website that you could use to extend your reach beyond your local community and open up the door for new clients and a new way of thinking (this also integrates the strategy of staying on top of a trend). As a go-getter, that advertisement makes you curious about getting your presence on social media and extending your network but, let's also pretend that you're a little on the older side and you're not so experienced with technology. Would you be willing to pay for that coach to teach you how to get set up? The answer is more than likely yes, because you know that whatever investment the cost of the class is, there is a lot of potential for you in the turnaround. One of the smartest things that you can do in life is to learn from the experiences of those who have come before you and to not repeat their mistakes! If you are using the right resources, the small investment you make up front in learning can save you months of aggravation and thousands of dollars in the long run!

Here is an excerpt from my Marketing book, which shows the different hot spots for people in general. Reviewing this can give you a good idea of where you can zero in on peoples' wants, although you should always analyze your individual clients on a case-by-case basis for the best results:

Put Consumers in Control

Control is a powerful thing to have. Who doesn't love being in control of things, especially when most peoples' lives seem to be out of control. By marketing your product or service as something that can give your consumer a sense of control, it may serve as a powerful selling point. In general, people like to be in control of their finances, personal safety, health, jobs, relationships and self-esteem. Furthermore, selling insurance on your product or service can also give the consumer a sense of control. Think about the last time you purchased an expensive item (maybe a new laptop or a set of new tires for your car) and you were asked if you wanted to pay extra for insurance purposes. People like knowing that they can get the most support out of their buck. If your product or service can provide consumers with a sense of control, it can be a very powerful idea to market it under that category and give them a sense of security.

Get Them through Their Family Values

Family is something that the majority of people value in life. For example, think about Disney World: people go to that theme park for rides, food, games and more, but what distinguishes Disney World from any theme park? The difference is that many people think of Disney world as a place to spend time with family. There is something for everyone in a typical family to enjoy. Focusing on family values can also stimulate memories in adult family members, which can make them more likely to buy something that they can share with their own family. Kids can be a big target for marketers, as kids are usually the center of most families. Marketing products as "kid friendly" can be a great selling point for getting a whole family to buy in. Depending on what you're selling, see if you can work in a kid-friendly version to help boost sales.

Pique Their Interest and Make Them "Discover" Something

Many people think of things such as outer space or animal science when it comes to the word "discovery." Who makes discoveries every day? You may think it is just scientists or researchers. However, for the little-name consumer, a discovery can be a breath of fresh air from the boredom of everyday life. Additionally, when a consumer discovers something about a product or service, they are more likely to tell others about it, which can give your company some free word-of-mouth marketing. When a person discovers something, it also helps them feel smarter, which in turn can boost one's self-esteem. Discoveries for a consumer often come in the form of a new idea or a new and improved way to get things done. If your product or service falls into the category of something that is helpful to your consumer and/or it can benefit their life, this can be a good way to market it. Use key words that promote a change that can happen in the consumers' life. "New" is a keyword that often works well and piques interest. Be sure to tailor your sales pitch in a way that lets the customer know what is new or interesting about your product or service.

Promote Fun and Laughter

Life can be very boring without some fun, games and humor. As the popular sayings go, "life is too short" and "laughter is the best medicine." Consumers are often looking for ways to have fun, so if you market your product or service in a way that promotes a good time, you may have an upper advantage. Promoting your product or service as "fun" is also a good way to help eliminate boredom from your consumers' lives. Even if your product is not really "fun", there are still ways to integrate fun into it. For example, you could create a small flash game to put on your website about your product or service to promote the concept of fun. Another idea is to give your product a humorous name or do something that goes against the norm. You could also make your product interactive. For example, if you were manufacturing different BBQ sauces, you could make your labels "scratch and sniff" to let consumers smell the flavor before they even taste it. Cartoon and animated pictures work good as well.

Market Your Product as Scarce

When your product or service is hard to get, there is usually a higher demand. Scarcity often translates to exclusive. Consumers tend to pay top dollar for something that is unique and not easily accessible. If everyone has it, the demand may not be as high. I just saw a show about the most expensive cars in the world, and this one company will only release 9 of its cars to the USA per year, and the starting price in 1.2 million all the way up to 1.8 million dollars! It just doesn't seem as fun if everyone else has it! Use keywords such as "last chance" or "if you don't buy it now," to create a sense of scarcity. Digital clocks counting down the time to the end of the promotion is hot right now as well.

Romance and Sex Sells

As the old saying goes, "sex sells" because it invokes such a powerful emotion in consumers. Humans possess a powerful desire to be loved and to love. Though men and women interpret this in different ways (women love the emotional, affectionate aspect and men tend to love the sexual aspect of it), romance and sex serve as a great selling point in marketing. It is important to remember not to be too over-the-top when it comes to using sex and romance. Don't give it all away but invoke peoples' curiosities and fantasies, so to speak. I am sure you have seen this strategy used a million times already, so need to elaborate much further.

Market in Terms of Self-Expression

As a part of self-achievement, consumers often express themselves through products. For example, Red Bull once had the slogan "it gives you wings," which was meant to signify energy, strength, endurance and a high athletic ability. Consumers who wanted to see themselves in that light would decide to drink that product. Similarly, people who drive expensive cars may see themselves as successful and people who think of themselves as entrepreneurial may wear expensive clothes or buy fancy houses.

Use the Desire for Self-Improvement to Your Advantage

Humans are often changing and "reinventing" themselves in some way. To your advantage as a salesman or business owner, the world is always changing, which leads to a change in living. If your product or service can serve as a self-improvement tool in some way, use it to your advantage. Make your consumers feel powerful enough to take that first step toward a new life. Present yourself as a coach or an expert who is ready to support the consumer in any way possible. Don't forget to work goals into the mix, as goals often motivate most consumers.

Target Their Self-Esteem

Self-esteem is a big selling point in consumer psychology. Everybody wants to feel good and many people try to achieve that status by buying things that make them feel prestigious and important. Good marketing can be achieved by targeting your consumer's self-esteem needs—mostly the desire to fit in and sit high on the totem pole. To market your product or service as "elite" or "prestigious," there are a few things you will need to do beforehand. First, your company or business must stand out from all the rest in its industry. Your consumers have to perceive you as better than the rest because many people will not have a problem paying more money for something that they think is more high-end. Secondly, don't underprice yourself. A lot of people who are just starting out think they can get more business by under-pricing themselves and looking more affordable. However, it is true that people get what they pay for and many are willing to pay a higher price for something they perceive to be quality. You could honestly be the best deal in town, but many people feel safer paying just a little bit more if they feel it will suit their needs just a little bit better. So be sure not to price yourself too low. Another point to consider is to take advantage of your product's aesthetics. Consumers go crazy over gold logos, high-end fabrics, and exquisite designs because it allows them to show-off. A great trick that many huge companies and others will do is that they will spend an extra dollar or so on making the package the product comes in extra special, and in return they have no problem charging quite a bit more as profit!

Save Them Time

Time is precious and there are only so many hours in a day. If you can market your product or service in a way that can save consumers time, you may have a powerful selling point. If your product or service can make the lives of your consumer more efficient, you absolutely cannot forget to make that known. When it comes to actually marketing your product, see if you can actually show your consumer just how easy it will be for them to save time with your product or service. Try to bring together different aspects of life that take up time by marketing your product in a way to kill two tasks at once. Focus on any aspect that can save your consumer time, steps, organization, or anything else that takes up a part of the day.

Knowledge is Power

The desire to be smart and knowledgeable is another hot spot where you can market your product or service to consumers. Humans believe that the more they know, the better decisions they can make and that is why knowledge is high in demand. If your product or service is not something that can help consumers learn something, you can still use this strategy to your advantage. Lay off the "selling" and just focus on informing your customer. This can help build trust between you and the customer and it makes the customer feel a lot more <u>confident</u> in his or her purchase. Make sure your website and any other content platform is well-written and contains informative information. Use seminars, videos and webinars to further educate your prospective and current consumers.

Research Companies You Will Be Dealing With

If you were ever unemployed and looking for a job, I will bet that someone out there told you to research a company before you applied and interviewed. Everyone knows that researching a company before you go in for a job interview is important because you can get into the mindset of the culture and sell yourself better. It's kind of the same thing as challenging the status quo except on a more large scale basis. Be sure to be prepared with the information that you need to persuade them as to why your company or product can benefit them.

By researching a company that you're going to be trying to sell to (and I mean hardcore research), you can give yourself a better chance of at least catching someone's attention, letting alone closing a deal. Don't just go on the company website and read the "company philosophy" or "mission statement." You won't find much information to work with there. What I mean by "hardcore" research is to really get up close and personal. Go on LinkedIn and see if you can check out the profiles of some of the people who work for that company—that can give you a really great idea of what kind of people you'll be trying to sell to. Look for group discussions, see what people are saying about the company and maybe even read up on the company history (that's a good place to pick up on company values). Don't be afraid to go in deep if it means you can have a better chance at a sale.

Of course, use common sense and don't overstep your boundaries. Don't come off as a stalker or a spy and don't start fishing for information too quick. See if you can somehow figure out how your profession is related to that company and try getting in on some of the group discussions you can find online. Start a casual conversation with an employee and take it from there. Try to make it as natural as possible without coming off as a pushy salesperson.

Ask Questions

Once you're face to face with a prospective client, be sure to ask questions. Think of yourself as a doctor who is in with a patient—as the doctor, you're trying to figure out the solution your patient wants for his problem. Good examples of questions to ask are things like "How are you currently running things," "Where do you want your company to be in x years," "How is your industry changing," "What does your plan look like," etc. As a salesperson that is not familiar with the way every company works, it is crucial to ask questions so that you can get a better feel for what you're dealing with.

A good strategy is to prepare these questions before your face-to-face meeting. This helps prevent any mind fog that may arise and it will help you appear to be more confident. Conversing with these basic questions is also a great way to make your prospective client feel comfortable around you and develop a good first impression—remember, the more comfortable your prospective client feels and the more they like you, the more likely you are to make a sale. Be sure to have all the benefits of your product memorized! I would personally make lists of all the benefits of the products I was selling and was always keeping a look out for new things to add to the list. You can even write down scripts for each part of your product, and then edit them for ultimate effectiveness and then memorize them! I used to do a lot of telemarketing, so a highly polished, well memorized script or just good idea of your product goes a long way! Just always remember to be confident and as helpful as possible.

The only important thing to remember when asking questions is this— don't do ALL of the talking and certainly take care to see that your prospective client gets to talk as well. Don't make yourself come off as too overbearing and try to keep the conversation as natural as possible.

Open-Ended Questions are the Way to Go

As you know, asking questions is important, but asking the *right* kind of questions is even more important. Think back to what I said about challenging the status quo—if people are having a problem, they will find a way to solve it and it's up to you as a salesperson to tap into their preferences. Ask questions that can stir up a conversation rather than get you a "yes" or "no" answer.

How many times have you opened the door to your cable provider's competition by them asking you if you're currently happy with the service you're receiving? Odds are you'll answer, "Yes," and that's the end of that. Or they may ask you, "Are you currently experiencing any problems with your current provider?" and you'll answer "No," and that's the end of that. The problem with yes and no answers is that it usually indicates the end of a conversation and nobody gets anywhere.

The key here is to ask different questions, even if they are not going to directly get you a sale in the first 5 minutes. Let's pretend your cable provider's competitor showed up at your door and asked you something like, "How long have you currently been with your provider?" or "What do you like about your current provider?" or some other open-ended question. The beauty about an open-ended question is that it will get you much more than a one-word answer and it will also give you the opportunity to see how your prospective client thinks. Once you've figured out how they think it can be much easier to pull them to your side.

Find out What's Going On in a Prospect's Life

When you ask the right kind of questions to your prospective client it opens up the opportunity for you to catch other selling points. One of the best ways to do this is to ask your prospective client about what's going on in his or her life. Usually life events such as a move, marriage, divorce, graduation, promotion, etc. can be used as a hot spot for upselling or getting your client to buy an additional product or service. For example, let's pretend that you work in the electronics department at a store and some of your bonus pay comes from commission. You have a customer come in looking to buy a new laptop. After asking the right questions, maybe in this case "What's caused you to need a new laptop," you learn that this customer is actually an upcoming freshman in college. You can now take this information and work with it...maybe by showing them the TVs you have on display or the graphing calculators or anything else that a freshman in college may need... more often than not, that customer will probably end up buying something other than what he or she originally came in for, especially if they think it will help them or that it is an upgrade.

Read Trade Publications

Sometimes the best way to get into the minds of your prospective clients is to literally put yourself in their positions. A great way to do this is to read trade publications. This way you can stay up to date on the trends that are going on in your prospective client's life, which gives you an upper advantage when it comes to catching their attention and talking with them.

Make the Most of Voice Mails

Although voicemail can be one of the most useful tools in modern technology, it is really scary to see that it gets underutilized way more than it should. When making a personal phone call, it is easy to assume that this person will just call you back when they see your missed call. In the world of sales it can be way different, especially since the person you're calling may not be familiar with you or your phone number.

The key here is to leave only one voicemail. I don't know about you, but I know there have been times where my phone has been bombarded over and over again. That's why when I did telemarketing I would go off very large lists and try not to overdo it. If a prospective client doesn't answer, leave a solid and clear voicemail explaining who you are and why you're calling. Don't forget to add a welcome invitation to get back in touch with you. Give him or her ample time to get back to you and don't call their phone over and over again—that will likely make them never get in touch.

Call Back Later

Let's say you've gotten in touch with a lot of prospective clients over the past year and they've declined your services. That's fine—but don't completely write these people off. Keep their names off to the side and then give them a call back a while later...maybe 3 months to a year... and call them to see if anything has changed. You never know, especially if you know they could benefit from your service. Over time people will get more familiar with you and thus, more likely to make a deal. You could also call these prospective clients just to see how they're doing, which can put you in a good position even further down the road. They may become unhappy with their current services at some point and then say, "Hey, that guy from company X or company Y called me that one time just to see how I was doing, I don't get that service with the current company I deal with." Next thing you know, you're closing a deal.

Body Language

Welcome Clients with Open Body Language

Standing with open body language can welcome a prospective client and make him or her feel more comfortable in your presence, thus increasing your chance of closing a sale. Open body language includes not having your arms or legs crossed, making eye contact and showing comfort in your clothes (such as removing a jacket). Speak confidently and show assertiveness without coming off as intimidating. Be sure you are well groomed, alert and armed with a great smile! Look them in the eye and be sure to let them know you would be happy to help them. People generally know within seconds whether they like you or not, so be sure to make a good first impression! I know you have heard that a thousand times before, but actually try making a sincere effort to do this and just see what happens!

Match Body Language to Establish Rapport

Much of the rapport you can build with a client can come off through matching his or her movements. This includes matching the way you're sitting, eye contact and even breathing patterns. When you can achieve rapport with a client, it makes the ambiance of the situation so much more open and comfortable. The more comfortable your client is, the more he or she is willing to like you, and the more you're liked, you have more chances of making a sale. This is an incredible strategy that really works! Almost no one will notice that you are mirroring them unless you take it too far. Be like people who are like them. If they tend to speak quietly, you can talk quietly as well.

If they are loud and aggressive, then you can be loud and aggressive as well if the situation permits.

Lean Towards The Prospect

When talking to your prospective client, sit in a way so that you're leaned in. Don't lean in too far, otherwise you risk invading personal space, but when done the right way, it can actually create a bond.

Sell With Subtle Movements

Using subtle body language can have a deep impact on making a sale. Subtle body movements can show a prospective client how you're feeling and it can even help you read your clients' minds. For example, a raise of the eyebrows can show that a person is feeling surprised and pressed lips can show that a person may be in disagreement with something you've just said. Generally, subtle movements that reflect negativity may be harder to pick up on than those that reflect positivity so you must teach yourself to be constantly aware. But if their arms are crossed, you can be sure that they aren't happy.

Attitude

Don't Complain

Complaining about the challenges that your job in sales can bring is a major thing to avoid. When you complain, you are equipped with a negative mindset, which can bring your willpower and determination down by a longshot, along with those around you. Instead, go into your job with a positive mindset (for example, think to yourself things such as "I can and I will achieve my sales goals!"). Your attitude is an incredibly powerful force! It was one of the reasons I was so successful. To truly have a grasp of the true power of a positive attitude, be sure to check out my book on Attitude.

Be a Leader

The best way to equip you with a strong and positive attitude is to be a leader. You don't necessarily have to have a leader's title. You just need a leader's mindset. Don't be afraid to try new things, go into "uncharted territory" or take risks—all of those things can make you a leader. The more that you regard yourself as a leader, the more likely you are to believe it and act upon it, thus increasing your chance of closing more sales. This will also grant the option of becoming a sales manager or achieving other higher positions in the company. There is too much to discuss in this one section, but if you want pro knowledge on how to be a great leader, be sure to check out my bestselling book on Leadership.

Be and Stay Competitive

Competition can be a fun thing. I know that I love being competitive. Competition can be looked at as negative, but in business you need to have that warriors spirit to thrive! It helps if you're a naturally competitive person (because these people are always looking to improve their game), but it is easy to become a little more competitive than you already are. A good way to do this is set some goals for yourself and then to find a friend or other person who can hold you accountable or compete with you on it. Then you can both work towards that goal and see who can reach it first or at the very least they can hold you accountable if you are not taking the appropriate actions. A good idea is to set up a reward for victory and a penalty for defeat, which is the classic style for getting results.

Stand Behind Your Work

There is nothing more powerful than a person (or company) that stands behind their work. Standing behind your work shows that you are confident, prideful and serious about what you do. It can also help you to establish trust with clients because they will be able to see how confident you are about your work ethic and the product or service that you're selling. Standing behind your work can also help build a positive attitude.

Don't Sell Too Early

The type of attitude you have can have an effect on your clients, too. One mistake that many people in sales make is that they try to jump and sell too early. Doing that may turn your client off and make you seem too pushy. Although you may be excited about the product or service you're selling (or nervous about closing the sale), be sure to contain yourself and focus on making a great impression rather than just trying to get what you came for.

Customer Service

Establish Trust

Establishing trust with your client is one of the most important things you can do as a salesperson. When your client trusts you, he or she is much more likely to buy from you. I saw a really good example of this on a message board once. There was a lawyer who specialized in defending those who were facing possession of marijuana charges. Naturally, everyone who was facing a charge was scared of what was to come and was looking online for answers to their questions. This lawyer had an account on a message board about the topic and commented on nearly everyone's questions. This made him look knowledgeable and passionate about his job and as a result, everybody wanted him to represent them in court— even people from other counties in the state were asking him if he was willing to travel. Clients want to know that the people they're doing business with are truly going to help them and be worth their time. There is no "right" way to establish trust—it differs for every industry, person and profession—but the goal is to make yourself come off like that lawyer did—passionate, knowledgeable and willing to help solve a problem.

You can increase your chances of establishing trust with your clients by putting all of the skills you're learning in this book together as you try to figure out what you need to do to accomplish that goal. Establishing trust is especially a challenge for those who are newer to sales because those who know the product better, who may have more experience and who have a long history of doing sales tend to have an upper advantage. People tend to trust things that have an established history— for example, look at how long Coca-Cola and Levi jeans have been around. That is because people know and trust them! One good way to motivate yourself toward this goal is to think about how much it will pay off when you actually do establish yourself.

Don't Rush Through the Sale

A few moments ago, I discussed why you shouldn't jump into a sale too soon. You should also never try to rush a client through a sale, either. This goes a long way with establishing trust. The reality is that nobody likes to be rushed, especially when they're taking the time to make an important decision. I know it's tempting to rush because you want to feel the satisfaction of a closed deal—but trust that it will be worth the wait, for both you and your client! There are a tremendous amount of returns every year from customers who felt rushed to make a purchase. Even if the product is not returned, often times the buyer will feel "Buyer's Remorse" and very unhappy with their purchase, maybe even leaving a negative review or bad mouthing you to their friends.

Practice Punctuality

Practicing punctuality may not seem directly related to closing a sale, but it can say huge things about you as a salesperson. Most clients have their own lives to worry about and nobody likes it when you waste their time—so if you schedule a call at 5pm, make sure your client's phone is ringing at 5pm sharp and if you have a face-to-face appointment at 3:45pm make sure you're there on the dot or 5 minutes early. Your client will appreciate it more than you know and help build trust between you.

Make a Custom Plan for Every Different Client

While having a basic sales plan is good, it is important to create a custom plan for every different client you have. No two clients are alike and what may work for one client may not work for another. If you are good at the marketing side as opposed to sales, you may be good at creating custom client plans. The important thing is to make sure that each plan suits your client and be sure to remember that the best way to design it is to figure out what your client wants.

Know Your Boundaries

If you can tell a client is getting uncomfortable, don't keep trying to push your way through to him or her. Slowly back off and allow them some space to form their thoughts. If you go over your boundaries, that's a sure-fire way to scare a client off.

Use Their Name in Opening Statement

Hearing your name is a powerful thing! It can make you feel important and exclusive because your name is the center of your identity. Using a persons name can help you capture your client's attention instantly. Simply say their name in your opening statement to set yourself up for a better chance of closing the deal. When your client hears you say his or her name, there is a better chance that he or she will feel more connected with you and trust you more.

Let Your Prospect Talk

One of the stereotypes of a traditional salesperson is that he or she does all the talking and doesn't let the prospect say anything. This can actually be a huge mistake! Let your prospective client talk— he or she will probably ask questions and make statements that you can use to infer what they're really thinking and which will help you explain to them why your product or service will benefit them. Allowing your prospective client to speak can also make him or her feel important and valued, thus leading to a better chance of a sale. Now remember this! When your client has run out of objections, questions or anything else to say... you need to recognize your opportunity and pounce like the pro that you are! **Give your closing line to seal the deal!** It is usually best to ask like this: So which option would you prefer: Option A or Option B? As a professional salesman, you need to know when to close!

Invite Prospects to Company for Observation

This secret probably doesn't pop into the heads of salespeople that often. Invite your prospective clients to come to your company for observation. Alternatively, you could invite them to a company event or seminar. This strategy can help build trust because it allows your prospective client to get a better grasp on what the company does and how it operates. He or she will see that your company is legitimate and not a scam or a fluke, like some sales companies tend to be.

Don't Push Product Right Away

When you meet up with a client, take a few minutes at the beginning of your appointment to settle in with each other. This can help your client become comfortable with you and you can both get to know each other. Don't immediately jump into the product or service you're trying to sell—that can make it look like you only care about making money and not about what your client's needs are.

Don't Make Assumptions about Your Clients

It's easy to make assumptions...everyone has been in that situation before. However, it is important not to do this when you're working in sales. As I mentioned before, no two clients are alike and you can end up surprised if you stop making assumptions. Assumptions about your clients can be limiting and may prevent you from many sales opportunities.

Marketing

Speak at Events/Give Speeches as an Expert

When people view you as an expert, they tend to trust you more. Positioning yourself as an expert is a great strategy for marketing yourself and opening up opportunities for sales. You can easily do this by speaking at events, attending networking sessions, getting an interview on the radio or anything else you can think of that would put yourself out there. You could also record yourself and put it on YouTube. That's a great way to reach many people at once.

Look for Referrals

Referrals are a great way to spread the word about you, your company and your products/services. Best of all, referrals are a great way to instill trust in clients. For example, let's say your client John had a pleasant experience with you and recommended you to his colleague Mary. Odds are that Mary will choose to do business with you because her colleague had a good experience.

Sometimes your clients will refer you automatically, but it is perfectly okay to ask for referrals if you're not getting any. A good and polite way to do this is to send out an email, either thanking your client or sending out an update and then mention at the very end that if he or she had a good experience working with you to please refer you. Some companies/salespeople even offer an incentive for referrals, such as giving a discount on their next purchase. This is something many peak performers in sales are masters at! If they can get a bunch of referrals from satisfied customers, it really makes the job so much more fun, profitable and enjoyable!

Follow up with Your Clients

Following up with your first-time clients can lead them to become your clients for life. In sales, people don't expect to maintain a relationship with the person who sold something to them. If you email or call a client on the phone not to sell something but just go "check in," you can leave lasting impressions. Your client will likely think to him or herself, "Wow this person cares about how I've been!" It's simply a feel-good move that can benefit both you and your client.

Keep Email Messages Short When Selling

Email is a great medium for selling and marketing your product or service, but only if you do it effectively. Since emails are composed in written word, it can be tempting to ramble on and on. As a writer, I know I can tend to write thousands of words on a subject! However, long emails can be hard on the eyes and your clients may easily become bored or uninterested if it's too long. Research shows that you have about 8 seconds to capture your audience and that's not a lot of time! The best types of emails are short and to the point—save the extra information for when you have a face-to-face meeting and let your personality shine in person. You can also let them know of upcoming sales, opportunities and much more! I personally use email marketing to give away my latest and newest books for Free, along with promoting some of the best life improvement products in the world.

Format Emails Correctly

Here's another big factor when it comes to successful email marketing — format your emails correctly! If you're typing directly into the email, it shouldn't be too hard to keep your text consistent, but if you're copying and pasting from another source, it can turn out to be a nightmare. Badly formatted emails are even worse on the eyes and are sure to turn off a reader within 2 seconds, maybe even sooner. Avoid big gaps between paragraphs and words, long hyperlinks, run-on sentences, punctuation errors and grammar. If you're including an image in the email, it may be a better idea to attach it rather than embed it because sometimes it won't show up on another platform.

Bad formatting should be avoided at all costs, but there are some good formatting tips that can actually make your email more captivating. For example, you could make the first line of your email slightly bigger than the rest to capture your reader's attention. You can also use bold font or different sized headers to break up the text so that your paragraphs are much easier to read and digest. In some cases, you might even be able to use different colored text to get your point across, (but don't go crazy overboard or it will have the opposite effect). If you want to include a link in the email, use a free link-shortening program such at Bitly to shorten the link (it keeps the email looking much 'cleaner' and you can check the statistics by logging into their website.').

Utilize The Subject Line for Email Marketing

In sales and email marketing, utilizing the subject line of an email is an absolute must! Why? It is because the subject line of your email will be the first thing your prospective clients see when he or she opens Gmail or Yahoo or whatever email program people are using these days. Close your eyes and pretend that you're checking your email... would you be more likely to open one that had a subject line of "no subject" or one that had a line of "business opportunity" or one that had a subject line of "Increase your income in 3 simple steps," or one that had the subject: "The solution you've been looking for all along," or anything else along those lines that could make its way into your target audiences' mind.

Make a Website

You might not think that a website would do any good for marketing your sales, but think again. The general purpose of a website is to provide your prospective clients with more information that can help them conclude whether they're interested in doing business with you or not. You should include several sections on your website, including a biography, some testimonials and your contact information. Most successful websites also have blogs, photo galleries, links to videos and product showcases. You can create a professional website at Wordpress.com or search for one of the many free website hosting services. You can also hire professional designers on freelancing sites such as Odesk or Elance, which is what I did, if you really want to personalize your website at a fair price. Feel free to check out my website to see what I did fairly inexpensively with some professional designers that weren't too expensive: www.AcesEbooks.com I'll admit it wasn't easy, but once you get it done, it is really a great feeling and it really helps with sales and the trust factor! Also, be sure to get a mailing list going as soon as possible. I personally use mail chimp, but I hear A-weber and many other services are good as well.

Design an Elevator Pitch

You may have heard of an elevator pitch before. It gets its name because it's supposed to be a pitch that you could easily explain to somebody while you're riding an elevator (which isn't a very long ride). As you know from learning about email marketing, you only have a couple of seconds to catch a client's attention. Design an elevator pitch about you and your business that could easily capture the attention of a prospective client if you were just in an elevator for a short period of time. You never know when you'll run into somebody who could lead to another sale. To learn more about how to craft the perfect elevator pitch, feel free to check out this YouTube video: Creating Your Perfect Elevator Pitch by American Express.

Prospect Consistently

Another big marketing mistake that many people in sales make is that they don't look for prospects consistently. It usually goes like this: You spend all your time looking for clients and then you finally get one or two... so when you're dealing with those few clients, you stop looking for business altogether in the hopes that these are going to close. While it is important to focus on your current clients as best as possible, you shouldn't forget about your future clients. What happens when you're finished doing business with your one or two clients or if they suddenly realize that you don't have anyone to do business with at all and go to someone else? In sales, if you want to be the best of the best, you must never give up on trying to get new customers! It is never 100% certain that a deal is going to close, so be prepared!

Confidence

Keep Yourself Clean Cut

Confidence is a big part of success in sales and a major part of being confident is your appearance. Be sure to keep yourself clean cut if you're going to be working in sales. That includes keeping your hair nice, being clean-shaven, taking a shower every day and keeping yourself groomed overall. In sales, people don't like to work with those who don't keep their appearance up. A well-groomed, clean-cut salesperson tends to come off as more trusting than one who does not put much effort into his or her appearance. Think of it this way—the way you keep yourself reflects the way you work, so keep it clean!

Dress Sharp and Professional

Another part of your appearance is the way you dress. In sales, it is important to dress sharp and professional. For example, a male in sales might wear a collared shirt, tie and slacks while a woman in sales might wear a nice blouse, slacks and a matching coat. Dressing professionally reflects how you work as a salesperson. When your clients see your dress, it allows them to make assumptions about you and you want those assumptions to be good ones.

Wear Neutral Colors/Scents

Never overdo it when it comes to your colors and scents! While it is a plus to smell nice, be sure not to make yourself smell too strong. While that may not have a direct impact on your client's decision to buy, it can certainly make a face-to-face meeting unpleasant. Just think back to a time where you were around a person whose cologne or perfume was too strong. Also, try to keep the colors of your outfit neutral. Although it may be tempting to dress brightly to stand out, it may actually make you come off as obnoxious, which can have the opposite effect on your client as well.

Be Proud of Your Sales Career

Show your pride about your career! Being proud can make you come off as one of the most confident people in the world. When your clients see how confident you are when it comes to sales, it is likely to instill a feel-good emotion, which can then lead to an increased chance of business. Being proud of your sales career can also instill a positive attitude in you, which can serve as good motivation.

Fear

How to Handle Rejection

Fear is an emotion that everyone in sales has to face one day. From cold-calling to face-to-face meetings, most people in sales fear rejection. Nobody likes to hear the word "No" and in sales, your salary most likely depends on all "yes's." However, if you're going to be a successful salesperson, it is important to know how to handle fear and rejection, otherwise you may never reach your sales goals.

The most important attitude to have about rejection is to not take it personally. When a client tells you no, it is easy to think he or she said that because of something that had to do with you. It is important for you to erase this mentality altogether. You must accept the fact that you will hear a lot of "no's" in your sales career and that it doesn't have anything to do with you. For every "no" that you hear, think about all the people who will say "yes" who are still out there, waiting to hear from you.

Additionally, just because somebody tells you "no," it does not mean that it's the end of your business relationship forever. Never burn your bridges or otherwise take any actions that will offend or scare your prospective clients off. There is always a chance that he or she will experience a change of mind and want to do business with you at some point in the future. Always end your interactions on a positive note and make it clear that he or she can freely contact you in the future.

Finally, rejection can be a huge learning experience for you. If a client has rejected you, you can reflect on the situation to determine how you could have done better. Did you use the wrong tone of voice or body language? Did you come off as too pushy? Did you focus on the client enough? Be objective and honest with yourself when making this evaluation and be sure to learn from your mistakes. If you think that your fear is holding you back in your career or in your life, be sure to check out my book on Overcoming Fear as well as trying out some of the great downloads from Hypnosis Downloads, they have some great audios that deal with overcoming all sorts of fears!

Self-Discipline/Personal Life

Know Your Goals

Goals are your #1 friend in sales! If you don't set goals for yourself in a sales career, it is very unlikely that you will be successful. "Sales" is a very competitive profession and one that cannot be taken casually. You cannot just have an attitude of, "Oh I'll make a sale when I make a sale." You absolutely must set goals for yourself. Your goals will act as your roadmap to victory. An example of goal-setting for sales can be trying to close 10 deals in a month or trying to gain 3 referrals per client. Your goals will give you a clear definition of what you're looking for and can help you tune your actions so that you get there.

Once you begin achieving your goals you can set even more challenging goals for yourself. As long as you keep achieving each goal and heightening the challenge every time, you can easily improve yourself as a salesperson and as a successful person in general. Always shoot a little higher than what's easy (but don't make your goals unattainable). Challenges are fun and exciting and are definitely great for keeping your mentally sharp!

Start Each Morning with a Positive Mindset

Remember how important <u>attitude</u> is? The best time of the day to set up a positive attitude is in the morning. Starting each morning with a positive mindset is the perfect way to make the most out of the entire day. From the moment you wake up, think of positive thoughts such as "Today I am going to work really hard to reach my goals," or "Today I will try something new/risky." It might not seem like it will make a huge difference, but your attitude often has everything to do with how your day turns out! Be sure to eat healthy in the mornings, don't check your email immediately, stretch out, watch uplifting videos, review your goals, exercise, and do what you need to do in order to perform at your best for the rest of the day! If you can do this consistently, you will make this into a powerful success <u>Habit</u> that will go a long way towards helping you be the best you can be! I personally started doing this about a year ago as of the time of the first publishing of this book and it has made a massive difference in my overall monthly performance! You tend to wake up excited and happy, because all you are doing is fun and invigorating things that actually help you succeed throughout the rest of the day!

Have a Support Partner

While sales can be a successful and a rewarding job, it is no lie that it can also be a challenging and stressful job. Sometimes, that can make going to work seem depressing, non-motivational and draggy. If possible, you should find yourself a support partner. It doesn't necessarily have to be someone else who works in sales— it can be anybody in your life who is supportive. Perhaps your support partner could be a close friend or a family member. Pick somebody who you can always count on to motivate you and help you see the positive side of things.

Set a Cold Call Quota/Per Day

Cold-calling can be a dreadful experience for some and that may cause you to avoid doing it altogether. However, cold-calling isn't always as bad and empty as it seems. A good way to get into the habit of making cold calls is to set a quota. A cold call quota can serve as one of your goals and you have the power to set it so that it can be as comfortable as possible for you. For example, if you're still new to it, you could set a monthly goal and then move into weekly and then daily goals once you become more experienced. Cold calling is a numbers game. You just have to grind it out until you find the nice customers who are friendly and who enjoy talking to you and who are happy to buy your service. As a former pro gamer and pro telemarketer, I can tell you that you just need to keep going, keep perfecting your script, keep perfecting your replies and sooner or later, if you are doings things right, you will be racking up the bonus sales. If you are working for a big name company, be sure to let the customer know this. One of my best sources of income during my sales days was contacting existing customers with my company and letting them know of new sales, specials or upgrades! They trust you immediately since they are already with you or your company.

Watch Your Numbers

Your sales numbers can say a lot about you, so always be sure to keep your eye on them. By watching your numbers, you will be more aware of how you stand. Knowing that information, you can determine whether you need to change anything in your selling strategy, keep doing what you're doing or decide if you want to experiment. If you don't know how well you're doing, it can be harder to know if you need to do anything differently. A masterful strategy many companies utilize is to post the sales prominently on the sales floor or in emails to everyone. I know it was always fun to be sitting at that number one spot for everyone to see! It was never easy, but it sure does drive people to try and be their best! Social pressure can be quite amazing!

Use and Internalize a Script

Having an internal "script" in your mind can definitely be helpful for when you run into prospective clients. If you're a shy person, it may be hard to start talking about your business and you may not know what to say to people who don't know you well. By coming up with a general script and rehearsing it in your head, you can be more prepared to talk about yourself on the spot. This can help you increase your chances of gaining more clients. Take your time coming up with the perfect script and practice it a few times every day so that you're 100% prepared.

Organize Your Life

An unorganized life can be a disaster for anyone— not just a person in sales. An unorganized life (for example, staggering bed times/awake times, unbalanced diet, unorganized home/office, etc.) can wreak havoc on your overall productivity and levels of stress. Bad productivity and stress levels can mean that you have extra, unnecessary things to deal with while you could be using that energy to focus on improving your game and increasing your sales.

Take a Break, Don't Work Straight Through

Breaks are an important part of your day, no matter what kind of job you're working in. I know it can be tempting to try and barrel through the day so that you can get all of your work out of the way, but trust me, that can actually kill your productivity! Always find time to schedule in a break. One good thing about working in sales is that you may have the flexibility to create your own schedule, so you may be able to decide if you want to take one long break or several short breaks. Have a snack, take a walk or do whatever it takes to help you recharge your drive.

Recite Positive Affirmations

Come up with a couple of positive affirmations that you can recite throughout the day or whenever you're feeling discouraged. This can help reset your mind to be back on track to your goals. This is just something that needs to be done if you truly want to be the best. You can come up with unique phrases or phrases that just make you feel good, such as: "I close easily and professionally." Or "I enjoy giving my product and services to those who can benefit." The possibilities are endless. Be a little Creative and come up with your own phrases that motivate you at this point in time to succeed! A good time to do this is when you are walking outside, in the car, or any other time you got some time to yourself. Do this for 10-15 minutes for maximum effectiveness.

Don't Be Afraid to Get Help

Never be afraid to ask for help if you need it. Nobody is born perfect and working in sales will take a lot of risk-taking, experimenting, trial and error, etc. Don't be ashamed to ask a person who is more experienced than you for advice or an opinion. Instead, think of it as a learning opportunity. If you have a manager, use them as a resource! Your manager's job is to help you succeed! I have had many terrible managers in my life, and luckily, a few great ones. So I know exactly what to do and what not to do when it comes to managing people. Your manager is surely going to hold you accountable, so you need to hold them accountable as well and make sure you are getting all the benefits and knowledge that you need. The right manager can make a huge difference in your sales career! If you have a terrible manager, it may be time to see if you can find a place where the grass is greener on the other side. Or, you can try to become manager yourself and lead your team to glory the way it should be done! I have personally made and broken the careers of many managers, so it is always wise to do what is right for everyone!

Chapter 2: Social Media Marketing For Sales

As the world is rapidly changing in technology, there is no longer a single need for traditional marketing methods such as snail mail, cold calls, general advertisements or similar methods. With the presence of connectivity, integration and social media websites, there is a whole other world out there that you can tap into to look for new leads and sales. This chapter will include several excerpts from my books on Facebook Marketing and Twitter Marketing to help you supplement your sales career and discover the great reasons why you should tap into these channels.

Reasons to Use Facebook for Business, Marketing and Sales:

Attract New and Current Clients

Facebook pages serves as a great way to attract new and current clients. Using this platform, you can connect with the people you already know (your current clients) and use your marketing skills to multiply your leads using the Rule of 52 theory. This theory states that for each person you know, they have 52 connections. If you can reach new clients through your current clients, you'll certainly be in good business.

Stir Up Clients

Your Facebook business page will also be a great way to stir up clients. In the next chapter, you will discover some awesome marketing techniques that can help you engage your audience, thus making the buzz around your business bigger. Once you have mastered that, you will have a great advantage in the world of Facebook.

Build Sales

By following the first two steps above, you can ultimately build sales for your business. Again, you will be able to learn more on how to do this with the marketing techniques in the next chapter. The more people you can reach on Facebook, the more potential sales you have in front of you.

Access Your Audience Any Time

Having a Facebook page for your business means that you can access your audience from anywhere at any time. Even if you're not in your business or office, you can easily check in with your audience on your phone while you're sitting on your couch. Establishing a sense of mobility means you can be more in touch with your clients.

Generate More Reviews

If you register your page as a local business, there will be an option for your fans to leave you a review. This can be hugely helpful to the success of your business because other people tend to follow the crowd. The more 5-star reviews and compliments you can get, the more likely your audience will be to trust you and use you. It is not easy getting reviews. I have heard numbers of 1 in 500 or 1 in 1000 will leave a review. You will have to actively ask for reviews in order to increase your odds. For a good example of this, you can see how I ask for your valuable 5 star reviews at the end of this book.

Private Communication

Not everybody uses email these days and it can be hard to find out your contact information if you're a busy business owner. Facebook pages have a messaging function which allows people to message you right through your page. This makes you more accessible (especially if you download the FB Page app to your phone) and your chances of driving sales increases more with better communication.

Better Customer Service

I have noticed some big companies use their Facebook page to their advantage when it comes to customer service. If a fan leaves a complaint or a bad review, you will have their contact information right in front of you, meaning that you can quickly and actively address their concerns. This can save you from losing a lot of customers, especially if they see you respond to them in a quick manner.

Personalize Your Company

By being able to type directly into your status update box, you can convey your voice to your audience. This makes your business much more personable and increases the likelihood of clients being able to relate with you.

Remotely Control Your Team

Since you can assign multiple users limited access to your page, you can remotely control your team. They can work from home as well and be able to access the page at any time. If you break up the task of managing your page among a few people on your team, it can greatly reduce the stress of your social media management responsibility.

Keep Your Audience Informed

Having a page for your business is a great way to keep your audience informed. Think of it like a newspaper that is specific to your business. As soon as you come out with a special deal, you can let your audience know right away as opposed to sending out snail mail.

Save Money on Marketing

Marketing these days can run pretty costly. Sending out mailers requires printing costs plus the costs of envelopes, stamps, delivery, etc. Radio and TV advertisements can be even more expensive. One of the best things about Facebook is that it is FREE! No gimmicks here, just a really great, free tool that is easy to use and allows you to access billions of people, literally.

Good Cold Call Replacement

If you're an introvert and not very good at making cold calls, use Facebook! You can still contact people by messaging them instead of calling them directly. This can also take the pressure off cold calls for both you and prospective clients. It can also ensure that you're not interrupting anyone's day.

Connects You around the Globe

Facebook is an international platform so anyone from anywhere in the world can access your page (if you allow it). This can be especially helpful for making international connections— who knows, you might end up opening a few branches or making a few leads in another country if you're a success.

Add a Link to Your Email Signature

Be sure to also add your link the bottom of your email signature. If you use Gmail, you can do this by going into your settings. Make it something simple and appealing. A good strategy is to put your name, then title, then link to your Facebook. This is helpful if you deal with a lot of clients through email. This is especially true if you work for a large and recognizable company.

Target Locals

If you run a business that has a physical store, you can focus on targeting people in the local area, which will help bring in more foot traffic. Combine this strategy with the Facebook Offers tool for the best burst of traffic.

Plaster Your Call to Action Everywhere

Inspire your audience to get moving and take action in terms of your business. You can put your call to action anywhere, including in your cover picture, at the end of your statuses, and in your paid ads.

Reasons to Use Twitter for Business, Marketing and Sales:

There is one marketing method on Twitter that is still slightly untapped. It does take time and effort, but the return can be amazing. The key is to become the solution to other peoples' problems. What do I mean by that?

Let's pretend that I am getting ready to market my latest self-improvement book but I am not sure how to go about it. What I could do is research the questions that people are asking online about the topic of the book. My latest book happens to be on leadership, so I will use that for this example. I could search for questions on any online forum, such as Yahoo Answers, but since this book is about Twitter I will focus on using Twitter. What I would do is find out who needs help with leadership. Then I would tweet them a solution—something about my book. If they are having leadership trouble, my book stands as a potential way out.

In the Twitter search bar, I would type in a short phrase about leadership and add a question mark at the end (signifying that I am looking for users who are asking real questions). For this example, I typed in "I want to be a leader?" After a quick search of the results, I found one young woman who expressed a concern about wanting to become a leader of alumni for her school. Now I have the option of reaching out to that young woman to make a connection and offer her a solution to her problem. Then I would go back and look for more opportunities. When doing this, try to experiment with the phrases you type into the search bar to get the most results.

Another method you can use is a type of networking—to try and get in with the "big time leaders" in your industry. This method is a little trickier and is not guaranteed, but it would be your loss if you didn't try it. What you can do is create a list of well-known professionals who have a big influence in your field. Research those people and try to connect with them on Twitter. If you can connect with them, try to build your relationship. One good way to do this is either research their personal website or Twitter account and mention something that they're currently involved in. Say something like, "Hey, I just wanted to say congratulations on your newest blog!" or "That's really cool that you're into x—I'm studying that myself," or something along those lines to build rapport. If they don't respond, try following through but don't be too annoying—give it two or three shots and if you don't hear back, move on and try to connect with someone else. As I said, this method can be a little harder to break into, but if you can do it, you can probably make some major connections within your field.

Now, there are some other things you can do to make that method much more powerful, and you are about to discover how!

Using Multiple Accounts to Boost Sales

If your business or service allows it, you can use multiple accounts to boost your sales. Managing multiple accounts may seem difficult but if you pair them up, you should have no problem keeping track of everything on a single platform. Using multiple accounts to boost sales is a powerful marketing method because it helps you reach more potential customers and it lets you branch off your business into multiple areas. For example, Starbucks has a main Twitter page for "Starbucks" but they also have separate accounts for their Pumpkin Spice Latte beverage, their career opportunities, and their public relations. This method is totally legal and is used by many huge companies, as you can see.

Driving Traffic and Sales with Hashtags

Do you remember how powerful the use of hashtags can be on Twitter? Not only can you use hashtags in a way to capture anyone who searches for a keyword, but you can also use them to market and promote your product or service. Many businesses hold contests in which they give something away in exchange for a tweet that contains a certain hashtag. When done correctly, this can help you product or service reach a huge audience. Just don't use too many hashtags in one tweet or for one account—then your audience may become too broad.

To make the most out of hashtags for your own product or service, use this action plan:

1. Create a spreadsheet and save it as a list of hashtags that are related to your business.

2. Search Twitter for existing hashtags. See if you can find all the relevant ones and copy them into your spreadsheet.

3. Use these categories to find hashtags: trending topics, content, events, location, lifestyle, and product.

Example: I am an author, so I would be looking to gather hashtags that are related to authoring and writing as well as the content of my books. One of the most trending hashtags that is related to writing is #amwriting. So if I was to send out a tweet about how I am working on my latest book and how I want my audience to be excited about it, I could post something like this:

Looking to improve your leadership skills? I am about halfway done with my upcoming book on: The Top 100 Best Ways To Be A Great Leader! Stay Tuned! #amwriting

With a tweet like that, I could reach anybody who searches for "amwriting," which is likely many since it's trending, and I could get my audience excited for the book before it even comes out. This works well for email marketing as well.

One event that I could tweet about is when my book goes free on Kindle, so I would use event-related hashtags such as #kindle and #free to let my audience know that there is an event happening where they can get my latest book for free, and then, of course, the hashtag: #leadership.

Lastly, I will give an example of a content-related hashtag tweet. Let's say that I am going to tweet about my leadership book. I could send out a tweet that looks like this:

Did you know that a great #leader often takes short walks to #destress? Find out why and more in my latest book, #Leadership [insert media].

Take a few minutes and see if you can come up with a tweet for each hashtag category that is relevant to your product or service.

Chapter 3: Closing the Deal

Now that you are equipped with the knowledge on the top 100+ things you can do to become a Pro salesperson, it is time to discover how to put it all together so that you can get a big "YES" and **Close the Deal!** This chapter will explain some of the best strategies that you can use to help increase your business.

Ask For Their Business

Simply ask the client for his or her business. Many salespeople believe that this can be rude or too pushy but, it's actually a very good but underutilized strategy. You don't necessarily have to wait for the client to approach you. Be straightforward and don't beat around the bush. If you're afraid of rejection, then work on overcoming it. In a sales career, those who can bounce back the quickest from adversity tend to thrive the most. Here are some good examples of how you can ask a client for his or her business:

"Just think about the great results that will occur on your end when we get the ball rolling. Why don't you and I get this up and running by the weekend? Which day is best for you to meet with me and sign an agreement? Wednesday or Thursday?

"Do you need to get the approval of anyone else for this? Are you ready to take this to the next step?"

"All you need to do is sign right here. Are you ready to do that?"

"When do you want to get your results by? Well then, why don't we get started today so that you can meet that deadline?"

Catch Your Own Mistakes

When I discussed how to handle the fear of rejection earlier, do you remember how I said it is important to learn from your mistakes? When it comes to closing a deal, it is doubly important to learn from the experiences that you had with past client interactions. Before you go to close a sale with a new client, it can be helpful to think back to your past few client interactions that got you a "no" and think about what you could have done differently. For example, think of anything you said or did that may have put too much pressure on your client. Think about your body language, your communication style and your overall strategy. It could be helpful to record your client interactions so that you can review them later on, but as always, be sure to get your client's permission if he or she is going to be in the recording.

Write Out a Contract

When you write out a contract, it makes a sale so much more real. It also allows your client to see the details of the sale in black and white, which can help establish trust. It also enables your client to ask specific questions and get a feel for what he or she is committing to. When you have a written contract to present to a client, he or she is more likely to accept the sale.

Using Price to Your Advantage

The price of the product or service you're selling can have a major influence on whether a client says yes or no. Therefore it is important to learn how to use the price of what you're selling to persuade your client into a yes. For this strategy you can focus on affordability. Ask questions that can help you determine how much your client is willing to pay or be able to afford. Then you can try to get your client hooked by showing him or her the costs that they can save or you can highlight the cost of *not* buying. If that doesn't work, try to remove any "extras" if possible and see if your client is willing to pay for the most basic version of the product or service you're selling. If all else fails, see if you can negotiate a more affordable price or, if you're able, allow your client to pay in installments. These can be situations in which you may be able to go to your manager and get a deal for your customer.

Give Your Client Options

People like to have options to pick from. Granted, you should not give them too many options (because that just makes their decision more complicated), but you should be prepared with some alternatives when it comes to closing a sale. For example, if you're selling a business service, you could present a couple of the packaging options to your client and ask "Which one of these seems like it can work best for you?" Options can include anything from different levels of service to different colors of a product. Customization is a desirable factor and it can definitely persuade clients to buy.

Give Your Client a Bonus

I'm sure you've seen those infomercials on television where the announcer says at the end, "If you place your order NOW, not only will you receive one but you'll receive 2 extra!" This technique works when making a local sale as well. People like things that are extra and free and it usually costs little for you to throw in something extra. Giving your client a bonus is a good way to invoke emotion. I used to close a lot of cell phone deals by throwing in a free leather case or a free car charger.

The Time Sensitive Close

In many sales cases, your client may say he or she will buy from you at another time. Unfortunately, the majority of those clients don't actually come back.

You can have a better chance of your client saying "yes" on the spot by making your deal seem time-sensitive. For example, you could emphasize on how limited your deal is or you could ask questions to find out what events in your *client's* life are time sensitive (for example a birthday or religious holiday) that could inspire him or her to buy. I had one client come in at the end of the month, and I convinced her to get 4 cell phones at the end of the day in exchange for a free leather case with each phone and with the managers approval, which also gave us 2 sales over the store in the neighboring city to give us the monthly championship! We had a lot of fun at the get together a few weeks later! Time sensitive deals can be very powerful!

Figure out Your Client's Emotions

As you know, emotions often play a big part in closing a sale. By asking the right kind of questions, you can figure out what your client is thinking/feeling and how you can use those emotions to get a "yes". For example, you could ask your client how he or she would feel if they had your product or service in their home right that very second.

Point Out Opportunity Costs

I touched on this briefly a few points ago, but pointing out the costs of *not* buying from you can sometimes encourage a client to buy for you. Your chances of this happening depend on the product/service you're buying, but it's definitely worth a shot, especially if you're selling something that can serve as a safety measure. For example, if you're selling piping insulation, you could say to a client, "Imagine if we got another blizzard and all your pipes froze and burst. If that happened, you'd have to pay thousands of dollars to get your pipes redone rather than if you just got them insulated."

Here are some other great YouTube videos that can serve as an awesome learning tool when it comes to closing the deal:

<u>Closing the Sale: 9 Common Objections</u> by Brian Tracy

<u>How to Close More Deals on the Phone – Young Hustlers</u> posted by Grant Cardone

Chapter 4: Building Your Sales Strategy

I bet you feel like a sales expert now that you have gotten this far! Now it is time to discover how to put it all together to get the best results for your business. I mentioned several times throughout this book that there is no one right answer, as sales is a broad career that differs across the board, but it is possible to create a guided outline that you can customize to your specific situation. In this chapter, I will help you to see everything more easily with a detailed sales strategy. Before I do that, let me share with you my favorite YouTube video of all time to put things into perspective for you: Six Secrets To Success (New) by Arnold Schwarzenegger posted by Travis Fisher.

The most important thing to remember when it all comes down to it is the 80/20 rule. The 80/20 rule suggests that 80% of your best results stems as a result of working on 20% of the most important tasks. For sales, this basically means that you don't have to use ALL of the tips, discoveries and strategies that you just learned about—you need to analyze your situation and decide which ones may work the best for you. Try and choose the top 5 that will work best for you at this point in time... and when those have been mastered, choose 5 more to work on. Just choosing to master ten of the best strategies in this book should not only help you in sales, but it should help you in life as well.

Here is a great way to get started:

1) Make a commitment to yourself to stay on top of the trends that are associated with your industry. This is a must for staying on top of the sales game no matter what you're selling. Remember that trends often fall off after a while, so this is going to have to be a persistent thing. It can be hard work to stay on top of trends, but the payoff is worth it.

2) Next, it is important for you to analyze your target market audience to figure out what they want. Remember, it's not about what they need but what they *want*. A good way to do this is to create an ideal customer profile. Your ideal customer profile represents your typical customer. You can then use it to craft your marketing strategy. It can be easy to ignore this one bit of information... but don't! I guarantee you the top corporations in the world have exact data on what their ideal customer profile is!

3) Using your ideal customer profile, you can now figure out what it is that your clients want. Be sure to brain storm ideas that will be effective based on your new found knowledge.

4) While you're working on your marketing strategy, it is a good idea to get your social media and email marketing strategy prepared as well.

Remember, you want to be able to reach as many people as possible.

5) Once you have your marketing strategy together, I suggest researching your competition. This can help you come up with ideas on how you can get ahead— perhaps you might think of something that your competition hasn't already. You can also research how your competition approaches your target market audience and then go from there.

6) The sixth step that I suggest is to compile a list of questions that you can ask your prospective clients when you get the opportunity to talk to them. Remember how important it is to ask questions— not only can it help you get a better idea of how your client thinks and feels, but it can also make your client feel important. The kind of questions you'll ask will, again, depend on what you're selling and to whom.

7) Be sure to practice your Communication Skills every day. Focus on body language and verbal communication, even if it means practicing in front of a mirror or in front of a friend. Communication goes a long way when it comes to selling and closing a deal and poor communication skills are bound to hold you back.

8) Try to inspire yourself every day so that you stay motivated to achieve the results that you want. Again, this will differ from person to person but here are some great ideas on how to stay inspired and motivated:

- Create a corkboard of inspiring pictures, quotes, memories, etc and keep it in a place that you frequent, maybe your office or bedroom. If you want to be hardcore, the best in the word, and ready to take on all challengers, you can do this as well at: Goals On Track. I especially like the ability to load up any picture I want to my goals page.

- The internet is full of pictures that have inspirational quotes and beautiful scenery. Personally, I like to use these as the wallpapers on my cell phone, computer, and other areas to remind me about my goals and purpose every day.

- Many people are often motivated by their family because they want to be able to provide the best life possible for them. Always think about your family in all of the decisions you make and you are more likely to make and achieve good ones.

- Read feel-good, inspirational stories in the news every day and try to avoid the more negative ones. This can help you feel inspired to go out and create more positive things in the world.

- Visualize your goals. Research shows that when you write down your goals and visualize them you are more than twice as likely to achieve them! Once again, if you want to be Pro, you have to do what the Pro's do!

9) Keep yourself in <u>good health</u>. Try to eat and sleep right and exercise at least three times a week. The healthier you are, the better you will be able to focus on your goals and it is also good for a very good first impression.

10)   Finally, don't forget to craft a referral strategy. Remember how important it is to prospect consistently? Not asking for referrals is just another way to cheat yourself. Don't be afraid to go out there and reach for the stars!

Here are some more helpful YouTube videos where you can see some successful salespeople in action. Hopefully they can inspire you to do the same!

<u>The Bad Salesman</u> by Emi Acas (A reminder of how NOT to act!)

The Best Language to Use When Closing the Sale by DaveYohoAssociates

Selling Over the Telephone by Richard Mulvey

Conclusion

I hope this book was able to help you to become more aware of how to overcome the challenges of working in sales and how you can use the strategies within these pages to thrive and dominant! Sales can be a hard industry. The true challenge in sales is to help your clients abolish their stereotype of salespeople so that they trust you and want to do business with you for many years to come. By following the top ten strategies that you found the most helpful in this book, I hope you are able to revamp YOUR sales strategy so that you can look forward to going to work and live the life of your dreams. Never forget, some of the highest paid people on this planet are sale people!

The next step is to start experimenting with the top strategies that you think will benefit you the most. I would highly suggest taking the time to determine your goals and then taking the time to make a detailed action plan based off of those goals! If you do this, you will save yourself a lot of time and aggravation in the future and you will be sure to be a mighty force to be reckoned with for many years to come!

Finally, if you discovered at least one thing that has helped you or that you think would be beneficial to someone else, be sure to take a few seconds to easily post a quick positive review. As an author, your positive feedback is desperately needed. Your highly valuable five star reviews are like a river of golden joy flowing through a sunny forest of mighty trees and beautiful flowers! *To do your good deed in making the world a better place by helping others with your valuable insight, just leave a nice review.*

Thanks and Best of Luck

My Other Books and Audio Books
www.AcesEbooks.com

Business & Finance Books

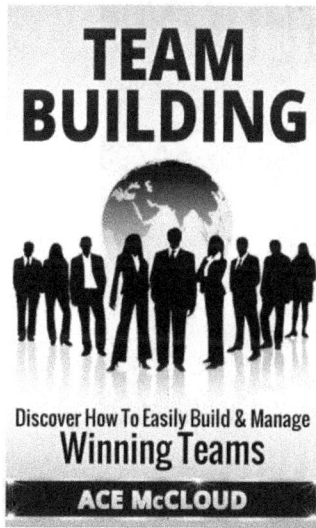

LEADERSHIP

THE TOP 100 BEST WAYS
TO BE A GREAT LEADER

Ace McCloud

MARKETING

The Top 100 Best Things That You
Can Do In Order To Make Money &
Be Successful With Marketing

Ace McCloud

FACEBOOK

THE TOP 100 BEST WAYS
TO USE FACEBOOK FOR BUSINESS,
MARKETING & MAKING MONEY

Ace McCloud

TEAM BUILDING

Discover How To Easily Build & Manage
Winning Teams

ACE McCLOUD

MONEY
THE TOP 100 BEST WAYS
TO MAKE AND MANAGE MONEY

Ace McCloud

TWITTER
HOW TO MARKET & MAKE
MONEY WITH TWITTER

Ace McCloud

COMMUNICATION
SKILLS

Discover The Best Ways To Communicate,
Be Charismatic, Use Body Language,
Persuade & Be A Great Conversationalist

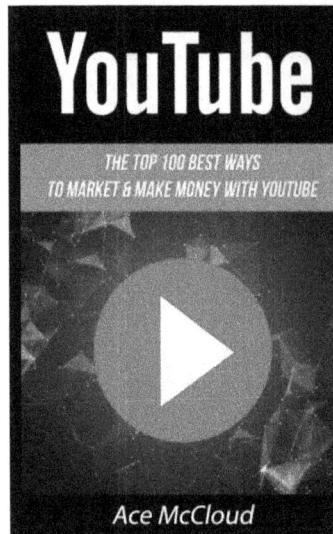

Ace McCloud

YouTube
THE TOP 100 BEST WAYS
TO MARKET & MAKE MONEY WITH YOUTUBE

Ace McCloud

Peak Performance Books

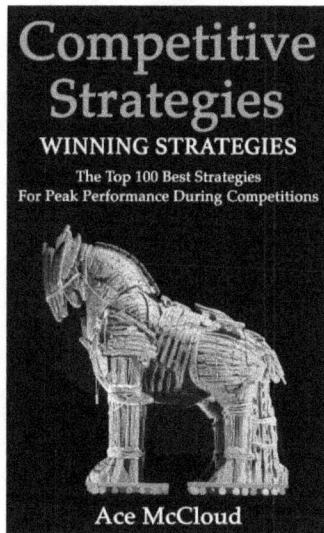

Be sure to check out my audio books as well!

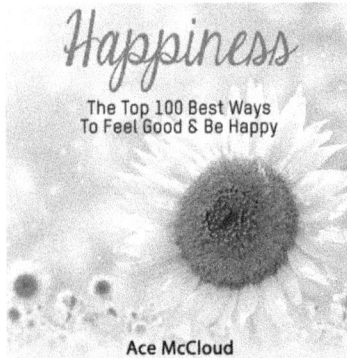
Happiness — The Top 100 Best Ways To Feel Good & Be Happy — Ace McCloud

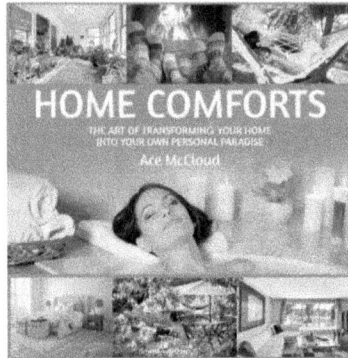
HOME COMFORTS — THE ART OF TRANSFORMING YOUR HOME INTO YOUR OWN PERSONAL PARADISE — Ace McCloud

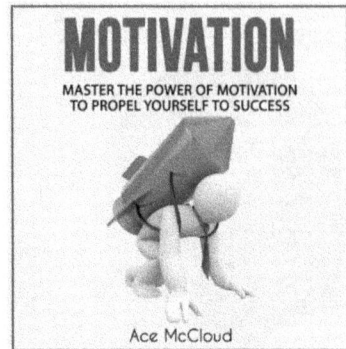
MOTIVATION — MASTER THE POWER OF MOTIVATION TO PROPEL YOURSELF TO SUCCESS — Ace McCloud

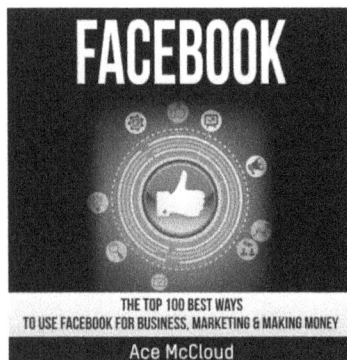
FACEBOOK — THE TOP 100 BEST WAYS TO USE FACEBOOK FOR BUSINESS, MARKETING & MAKING MONEY — Ace McCloud

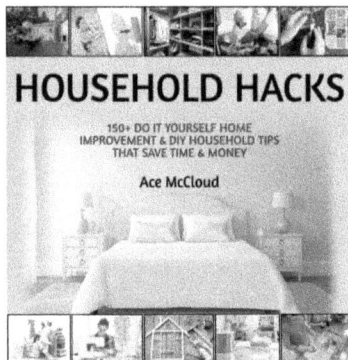
HOUSEHOLD HACKS — 150+ DO IT YOURSELF HOME IMPROVEMENT & DIY HOUSEHOLD TIPS THAT SAVE TIME & MONEY — Ace McCloud

SUCCESS — SUCCESS STRATEGIES — THE TOP 100 BEST WAYS TO BE SUCCESSFUL — Ace McCloud

Check out my website at: **www.AcesEbooks.com** for a complete list of all of my books and high quality audio books. I enjoy bringing you the best knowledge in the world and wish you the best in using this information to make your journey through life better and more enjoyable! **Best of luck to you!**